Ex-Library: Friends of
Lake County Public Library

The
North American
INDIANS

The Marshall Cavendish illustrated history of

The
North American
INDIANS

Homes, Food and
Clothing

MARSHALL CAVENDISH
New York • London • Toronto • Sydney

LAKE COUNTY PUBLIC LIBRARY

3 3113 01261 8791

Library Edition Published 1991

© Marshall Cavendish Limited 1991
© Pemberton Press Limited 1991

Published by Marshall Cavendish Corporation
2415 Jerusalem Avenue
Bellmore
N.Y. 11710

Series created by Graham Beehag Books
Produced by Pemberton Press Limited

Designed by Graham Beehag
Illustrated by Kerry Bridge
Edited by Maggi McCormick

All rights reserved. No part of this book may be reproduced or utilized
in any form or by any means electronic or mechanical including photocopying,
recording, or by any information storage and retrieval system, without
permission from the copyright holders.

Library of Congress Cataloging-in Publication Data

Oakley, Ruth,
  The Marshall Cavendish illustrated history of the North American
Indians / Ruth Ena Oakley. – Limited ed.
      p. cm.
  Contents: v.1, In the beginning – v.2, Homes, food and clothing – v.3,
A way of life – v.4, Religion and customs – v.5, Art and totems
– v.6, Conflict of cultures.
      ISBN 1-85435-137-0 (set)
  1. Indians of North America – Juvenile literature. [1. Indians of
North America.] I. Marshall Cavendish Corporation. II. Title.
E77.4.O18 1990
970.004'97–dc20   89-17371
                                                              CIP
                                                              AC

Printed and bound in the United States by Lake Book Manufacturing Inc.

Contents

The kinds of homes in which native Americans lived were determined by three main factors: the climate in the place where they lived, what natural materials and resources were available to them, and whether they lived a settled or a nomadic existence.

*Right:*Tepees on the reservation of the Umatilla tribe of the Great Basin photographed in about 1900.

Tepees of the Plains

The Plains Indians lived in tepees, which were large, cone-shaped tents. The framework of a tepee consisted of three or four large, strong poles. The men of the tribe made expeditions to a nearby forest to cut down trees to make these stakes. Depending on the size of the tepees, the poles could be up to about 25 feet long.

It was the women's work to put up the tepees. It took about half an hour to erect one. The main poles were lashed together at one end. Then, they were arranged to stand on end in a tripod shape. About twenty thinner sticks gave added support between the main poles.

Then, the outer covering of the tepee was laid over the framework of sticks. It was made of tanned buffalo hide and laced up with thongs of sinew. An ordinary tepee had a diameter of about 12 to 15 feet. For a large ceremonial tepee, up to fifty hides might be sewn together. They were usually beautifully painted and decorated.

There was a kind of chimney, an opening with a

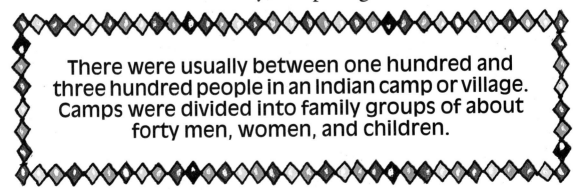

There were usually between one hundred and three hundred people in an Indian camp or village. Camps were divided into family groups of about forty men, women, and children.

Family life among
the Plains Indians.

funnel at the top of the tepees to allow the smoke from the fire to escape. The direction of the funnel could be adjusted according to the wind direction, so that the smoke could be cleared efficiently. The fire was lit in the center of the tepee. The head of the household sat behind the fire facing the door, which was a narrow opening with a flap of skin which could be closed.

The lower edge of the covering was held down tightly with tent pegs or stones. An inner lining was

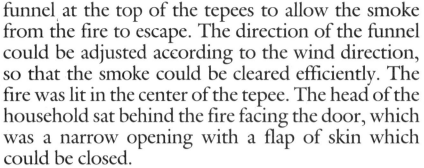

A pair of tepees joined together and a rack for drying eels on the Umatilla Reservation, Oregon, around 1900.

tied to the poles in winter to keep out the wind and drafts. In the summer, the bottom edge of the tepee was rolled up to let the air circulate.

When the tribe wanted to move to other hunting grounds, each family could easily dismantle its tepee. The poles were used to make a travois, a portable platform on which they transported the hide covering of the tepee, their goods, and their children.

In Canada and along the northwest coast, the Indians used tepees covered with birch bark.

Left: A tepee of the Yakima tribe which has a covering of rush mats.

Wigwams

Wigwams were similar to tepees. They were made from a framework of poles, but they had rounded tops. They were covered with woven mats or birch bark, not with animal skins. Small, very simple, wigwams were called wickiups. They were covered with dried grass or rushes and were found in desert areas like the Great Basin.

The Indian tribes who lived along the northwest coast of North America built large wooden houses. They used the natural resource of the large cedar trees which grow in the thick forests of the region.

Right: A Choctaw mother and children at the entrance to their wigwam.

The largest houses were built by the Coast Salish tribe. One Coast Salish house five hundred and twenty feet long and sixty feet wide stood near Seattle until 1900. It was so big that young athletes use to run races inside it.

These houses were usually built in a row, so that their entrances faced the sea or the river. Huge logs were placed upright in a rectangular shape and sunk into the ground deep enough to be rigid and secure. The tops of the posts were notched, so that logs could be placed on them horizontally to carry the weight of the roof.

Then, planks of split cedar were placed over the

A wigwam covered with moss and grass. A skin is being dried as part of the tanning process.

A "ramada" was a kind of veranda, except that it was separate from the house. The Navajo made them from four poles and a frame covered with brushwood. It made a shady, comfortable place to work or relax during the day.

framework to make the walls. Sometimes, the planks fitted into notches which were cut into the upright posts. Some tribes lashed them on with cords made from twigs or roots.

Planks were also laid on the ground to make a wooden floor. The roof was made of strips of bark or of planks.

This kind of house was very convenient when the tribe wanted to move to another area. They simply took down the planks and loaded them onto a pair of canoes to make a raft. They could then load their household possessions onto the raft and paddle to the next village site. There, they erected another framework of logs so that they could quickly make another house. Many tribes had summer houses and winter houses, so they could take advantage of the fish and game available at different seasons.

Several families lived in one house. Inside, each house was divided by partitions made of mats or cedar bark hung on rods. Beds were usually a series of shelves running around the walls. Each family had its own fire. As there was often no attempt to make a chimney or hole in the roof, the cabins were very smoky.

Sometimes, carved and painted totem poles adorned the entrance to the house, and the main supporting logs might be carved as well.

Long houses of the northeast

The homes of the Iroquois, who lived in the woodlands of the northeast, were covered with bark. The main structure was built from poles cut from the trees of the forests. A typical long house measured from seventeen to thirty (or more) yards long. It had a central corridor three or four yards wide, and a door at each end.

Each long house was occupied by up to twenty families, who were usually related. Each family had a compartment, and they shared cooking fires in the corridor. This made for a noisy, smoky way of life with no privacy.

The interior of a Mandan lodge with a roof made of earth. The Mandan lived on the Plains and Prairies.

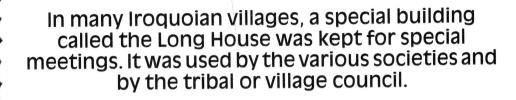

In many Iroquoian villages, a special building called the Long House was kept for special meetings. It was used by the various societies and by the tribal or village council.

Apartment buildings of the canyons

The Hohokam and the Anasazi, early tribes of the southwest, built their houses of bricks which they made from mud and dried in the sun. This material is called adobe. Caliche, which is dried, stiff clay, was also used.

The early pioneers nicknamed these building materials "prairie marble," because they are very strong and durable. In fact, buildings are still made of them today.

The Anasazi people originally built round, domed houses made of logs with mud between the cracks. Then, they made pithouses and eventually began building with stone and adobe above ground. Their descendants, who continued to build in the same style, were known as Pueblo Indians. Pueblo is a Spanish word which means "a town."

The Pueblo house was rectangular in shape and built either from stones held together with adobe or from bricks made of adobe. The roof was made of brushwood held together with mud. It was supported by rafters cut from pine trees.

Gradually, the Pueblo tribes began to join their houses together, either side by side or on top of one another, so that they were like apartment buildings. Pueblo Bonito in Chaco Canyon, New Mexico, consisted of a huge arc of dwellings up to five stories high and containing eight hundred rooms.

Left: The ruins of Pueblo Bonito. The circular buildings are kivas which were used for religious ceremonies and social occasions.

The Pueblos were agriculturalists, raising sheep and cattle and growing crops. They did not move around from place to place like the nomadic hunters and foragers of other areas, and so they built substantial permanent dwellings. They also continued to build pit houses called "kiva," not to live in, but for social and religious ceremonies. They were circular and were accessible only through a hatch in the roof.

As the tribes grew and prospered, they began to compete for available land. As competition increased, they needed to build towns which were easier to defend. They began to build homes located in the walls of the steep canyons of the region, such as the famous example at Mesa Verde in southern Colorado.

Below: A Hopi pueblo at Walpi, Arizona, photographed in about 1879.

Earth Lodges of the Navajo

The Hopi and the Zuni are two of the modern Pueblo Indian tribes. The Apache, the Comanche, and the Navajo came to the southwest later in history. They were very successful, and today, the Navajo are one of the largest tribes in the U.S.

The Navajo word for house is "hogan." The early hogans were cone shaped and made from sticks

A dome-shaped earth lodge on the Omaha Reservation, Nebraska. Corn hangs on a drying rack on the left, and the woman in front is pounding corn in a wooden mortar.

covered with earth. Today, the Navajo still build—and live in—earth lodges. The hogan is circular to symbolize the sun and the universe. Logs packed with mud form the walls. The wooden roofs are dome shaped and covered with hard, packed earth. A smoke hole is left in the middle of the roof.

When someone dies, the hogan is abandoned and a new one built.

Furniture

Most traditional Indian homes contained little furniture. The nomadic and hunting tribes would not want to have too many possessions to carry on their travels.

The family often slept on a raised bench against the walls of the house or tepee. They did not have mattresses and bedding, but wrapped themselves in warm robes made of animal skins when they went to sleep.

The Natchez of the southeastern woodlands, along the valley of the Mississippi River, slept on

Backrests made of slats of wood, which were used instead of chairs, are visible in this tepee.

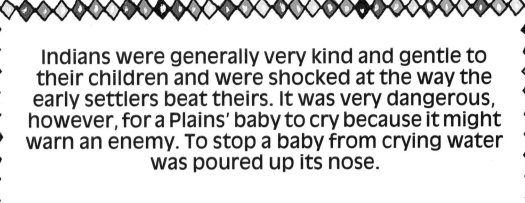

Indians were generally very kind and gentle to their children and were shocked at the way the early settlers beat theirs. It was very dangerous, however, for a Plains' baby to cry because it might warn an enemy. To stop a baby from crying water was poured up its nose.

mats which were attached to poles which rested on four notched sticks to raise them off the floor.

Instead of chairs, there were backrests made of woven willow twigs supported on a tripod of sticks, but most Indians were happy to sit on the floor.

In the wooded areas of the northwest and the northeast, tribes such as the Coast Salish and the Iroquois made wooden chests in which they stored their personal belongings and food.

The floor and walls of most dwellings were covered with woven mats or animal skins, and religious objects, and those thought to possess magical powers, were hung on the walls.

Fire

A fire burned night and day in the center of the dwelling. It provided both warmth and a means of cooking. It also symbolized the sun as the source of life, so it was regarded as sacred by many tribes who always kept it burning.

The Natchez and the Iroquois used fire to clear sites for planting in the woods. They lit fires around the base of trees which they wanted to fell. Saplings were used to make a platform around the tree about three feet off the ground. Then, wet blocks of sod were placed on the platform close to the tree. When fires were lit under the platform, the flames were concentrated around the base of the tree to burn it away. It was then much easier for the Indians to cut down the trees with their stone axes.

Once they had felled the trees, the Natchez also used fire to help them hollow out the trunks of poplar and cypress trees to make dugout canoes. The fires burned away the top of the trunk, so the charred remains were much easier to shape. The fire could be controlled by strategically placing damp clay in the right spots to produce whatever shape was required.

Lacking the convenience of a box of matches, the Indians had several methods of making a fire. In pre-historic times, flint or lumps of iron pyrite were struck hard together to produce sparks, which fell on dry leaves, grass, or bark and set them alight. Another method involved rubbing a pointed stick very rapidly in a twisting motion inside a notch in another stick. This action causes friction, and the heat generated builds up until it sets fire to some dry material as before.

A more modern device for firelighting consisted of a bow which rotated the fire stick by twisting the bow string around the middle of the stick. The bow

There was often a palisade of poles around an Iroquoian village to defend it. Sometimes the poles were thick and close together, but sometimes they were only three inches thick and a foot apart. Perhaps the latter had brush woven between them or sheets of bark fastened to them to make a fence.

Making fire.

was then moved steadily backwards and forwards with the point of the stick in a hole drilled in a special stone.

The Iroquois also used a pump drill for making fire. When one fire was alight, burning material such as bark or dry moss was carried from one home to another in an animal horn or a pot. This provided a quick and useful method of starting fires, particularly when setting up a new camp.

Carrying fire in a horn.

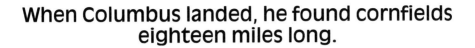

When Columbus landed, he found cornfields
eighteen miles long.

Boiled caterpillars eaten with salt were a great
treat to the Yahi of Southern California.

Food

The Indians' diets differed according to their life-style and location, but it was generally healthy, balanced, and varied. For most tribes, the food supply was erratic, depending on the season. All tribes developed methods of storing and preserving food from the times of plenty. Nevertheless, there were times of great hardship, and even starvation, for many tribes. Some tribes, such as the Cree, even had to resort to cannibalism in these circumstances.

The nomadic hunters ate mainly meat, and the farmers and foragers enjoyed a wide range of cereals, fruits, nuts, and vegetables. The most important staple food among the agriculturalists was corn. There were many varieties; including flintcorn in the northeast and on the Plains, dent corn in the southeast, flour corn in the southwest; and sweetcorn, popcorn and pod corn.

Many kinds of beans, squash, pumpkins, melons, potatoes, tomatoes, fruits, peanuts, and cashew nuts were also cultivated.

In addition to making the most of their cultivated crops, the Indians were also adept at using local natural resources. Children and women gathered wild rice, currants, strawberries, wild plums, and many other berries and seeds in the countryside. Honey was taken from bees' nests after the insects

Harvesting maize.

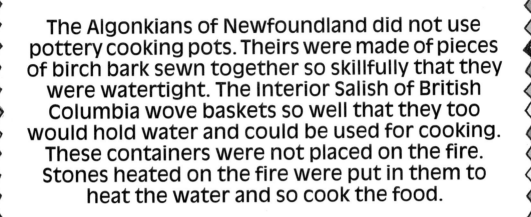

The Algonkians of Newfoundland did not use pottery cooking pots. Theirs were made of pieces of birch bark sewn together so skillfully that they were watertight. The Interior Salish of British Columbia wove baskets so well that they too would hold water and could be used for cooking. These containers were not placed on the fire. Stones heated on the fire were put in them to heat the water and so cook the food.

had been smoked out. The Iroquois made maple syrup from the sap of the local maple trees.

Along the Pacific coast, acorns were a staple foodstuff. Acorns are bitter because they contain natural tannic acid. To counteract the strong taste, tribes such as the Chumash, the Hupa, the Pomo, and the Yurok of California ground them between stones to make a meal which they then washed repeatedly in a stream.

The Iroquois gathered walnuts, hickory nuts, butternuts, and beechnuts as well as acorns. Small animals and insects, such as locusts, ants, and caterpillars, were also enjoyed as free food sources.

The hunting tribes ate any game animals that were prevalent in their area. The northeastern tribes such as the Algonquin, the Micmac, the Ojibwa, and the Cree ate moose, caribou, deer, porcupine, hares, beaver, and bear. They also caught fish and shellfish, and the tribes who lived near the sea hunted seals and white whales. Ducks, geese, grouse, and ptarmigan were also enjoyed.

On the northwest coast and in British Columbia, the food was similar, with the addition of salmon, cod, halibut, and clams. Seaweed was a prized delicacy. Salmon and clams were stored for the winter. They were smoked over a slow fire and dried to pre-

Some of the wild plants and animals which the Indians used for food.

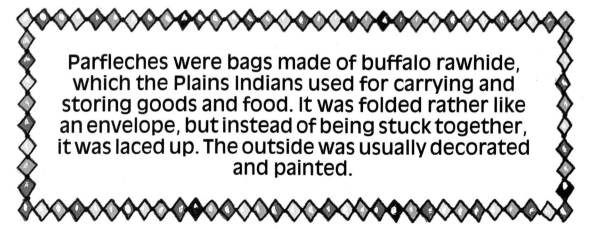

Parfleches were bags made of buffalo rawhide, which the Plains Indians used for carrying and storing goods and food. It was folded rather like an envelope, but instead of being stuck together, it was laced up. The outside was usually decorated and painted.

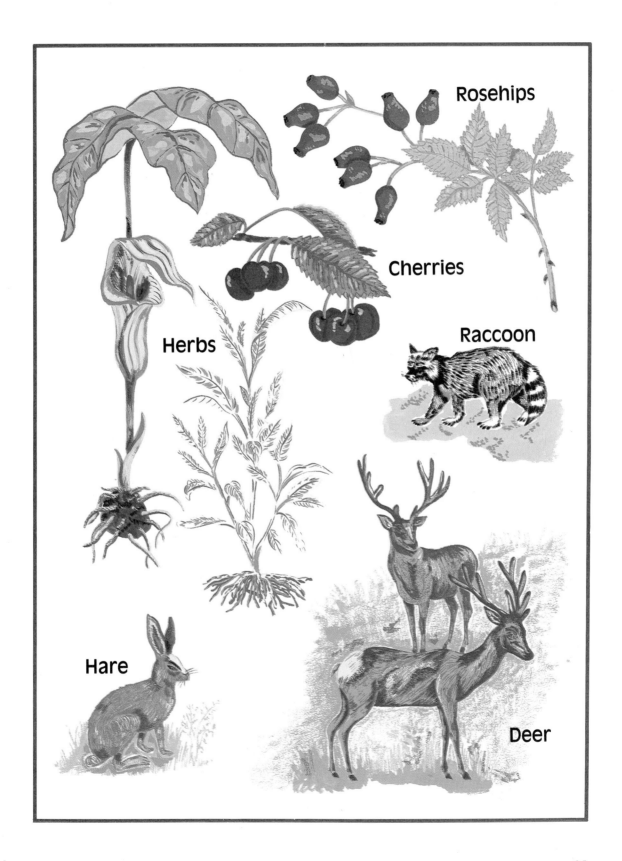

Rosehips

Cherries

Raccoon

Herbs

Hare

Deer

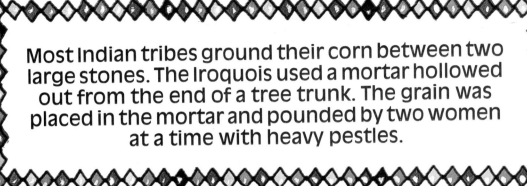

> Most Indian tribes ground their corn between two large stones. The Iroquois used a mortar hollowed out from the end of a tree trunk. The grain was placed in the mortar and pounded by two women at a time with heavy pestles.

Hopi girls in Arizona grinding corn.

serve them. Seaweed and berries were pressed into cakes and dried.

In some areas, meat could be kept frozen in the winter. It was stored in caches, which were actually little log cabins in the trees. Sometimes, the bark was stripped from the tree to make it too slippery for animals such as the wolverine to climb and steal the food. The animals were very persistent and crafty, however. They always managed to steal some of the precious stores.

Alternatively, food could be stored in pits dug in the ground and lined with birch bark. The Iroquois stored their grain and roots in wooden chests in their houses.

The inner bark of some evergreen trees and poplars was collected with a special tool made from thin bone or an antler. The strips were soft and juicy and tasted of orange.

> The bulb of the camas, which is similar to a hyacinth, was eaten by Indians who lived on the Plateau. It was boiled, roasted, made into cakes, or eaten raw.

For the Indians of the Plains, the buffalo was the main source of food. The meat could be eaten fresh, or it could be smoked and dried. Fresh meat was either roasted on a spit over a fire or made into a stew which was boiled in a bag made from the stomach of the buffalo itself.

Often, the meat was dried. Lean meat was cut into thin strips, which were slit and hung on racks to dry in the hot sun. When the jerky, as it was called, had dried out completely, it could be stored until it was needed. Then, it was softened in hot water or eaten dry.

Another common, very useful preserved food made from dried buffalo meat was pemmican. To make it, the women of the tribe laid a buffalo skin on

the ground and put a large, flat stone in the middle. A slice of dried meat was placed on the stone and hammered with a smaller, rounded stone until the meat became like powder. Hot buffalo grease was poured over the powdered meat, and the ingredients were mixed together.

Pemmican was stored in tightly sewn bags made of animal hides. It would keep for several years if necessary. It provided a nutritious food which was easy to carry and could be eaten cold or cooked, or made into soup. Sometimes, berries, cherries, or peppermint leaves were added to the mixture. Pemmican could be made with the meat of other animals as well, and some Canadian tribes made fish pemmican.

Plains Indians hunting buffalo on horseback.

Cooking

Food was cooked in three ways. One was to dig a pit in the ground, line it with stones, and light a fire in it. Food could then be placed in the pit and cooked. Another method was to hang food over the fire on a spit. The third method used large containers made of birch bark, clay, wood, stone, or tightly woven baskets. These pots were filled with water, and red hot stones were dropped into the water to heat it and thus cook the food. The Indians made their containers from the materials which were most readily available to them. After trade with the white settlers began, they began to use metal utensils as well.

Right: These women of the Papago tribe were photographed in 1916 preparing food. One is cooking cakes inside the corn-husk shelter; the other is scraping corn into a basket.

Below: A woman of the Taos tribe baking bread in a "bee-hive" oven.

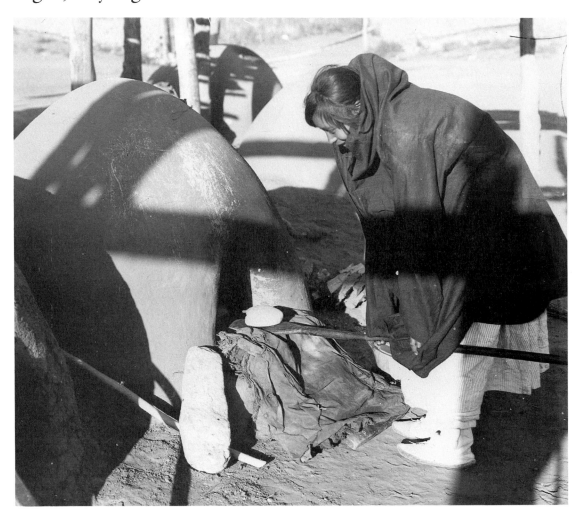

Clothing and fashion

For most Indians, the animals which they hunted provided their clothing as well as their food. The climate in their territory dictated their dress: the farther south they lived, the fewer clothes they needed to keep warm. Like most people, however, the Indians used clothes, jewelry, and facial and body decoration for adornment as well as for practical reasons.

Tattooing

The southernmost tribes and the poorer ones, such as those in the Great Basin, wore hardly any clothes except a breechcloth for the men and a skirt for the women. They tattooed themselves all over or painted themselves with colored muds and minerals. Tattooing was also common in northern Canada and among the tribes of the Pacific Coast.

It was a very painful process and was regarded as a sign of courage. A half-breed, who had experienced both, reported to an early explorer that having an arm amputated was less painful than being tattooed. On the face, the tattoo artist carefully inserted an awl under the top layer of a person's skin. Then, a piece of cord dipped in dye or charcoal was pulled through the channel which was made. A frame with needles of various sizes set in it was used for tattooing the body. The frame often had bells attached to it to cover up the groans of the person being

Right: A tattooed Timucua chief in Florida consoles mourning widows in this engraving of a sixteenth-century eyewitness drawing by the French artist Jacques le Moyne.

Natchez men plucked out their beards, eyebrows, and body hair with clam shells or copper tweezers.

tattooed. The process could take three days to complete. Men tended to be more heavily tattooed than women, who generally had just a few lines on their faces.

Face and body painting

Face and body painting was not permanent; it was sometimes done just as decoration, and sometimes as part of a religious or secret ceremony. Many different colors could be made using vegetable and mineral dyes.

Indian warriors displaying their body painting.

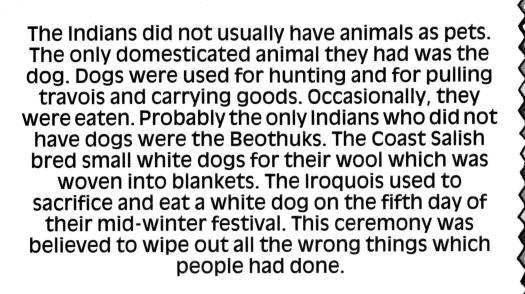

The Indians did not usually have animals as pets. The only domesticated animal they had was the dog. Dogs were used for hunting and for pulling travois and carrying goods. Occasionally, they were eaten. Probably the only Indians who did not have dogs were the Beothuks. The Coast Salish bred small white dogs for their wool which was woven into blankets. The Iroquois used to sacrifice and eat a white dog on the fifth day of their mid-winter festival. This ceremony was believed to wipe out all the wrong things which people had done.

Hair styles

Indian men usually took great pride in their appearance and were as careful about their hair styles as they were about their body decoration and clothing. Hair was usually worn long; members of the Crow tribe wore it in two braids which were artificially lengthened. The Pawnees shaved their heads, leaving a long scalp-lock hanging down the back from the crown of the head or a strip of hair down the middle of the head like a brush. In other tribes, mud and grease were used to stiffen the hair so it could be dressed in a particular way. These styles often indicated whether the wearer was married or unmarried, an untried brave, or a warrior. Indian men usually have little facial or body hair. In the past, they plucked out any hairs which did appear.

Women usually wore their hair long and parted in the middle. Some tribes reddened the part with ocher or vermilion. To keep their hair off their faces, women usually wore a head band or braids. In some

41

Left: A Hopi girl displaying a typical hairstyle of the tribe.

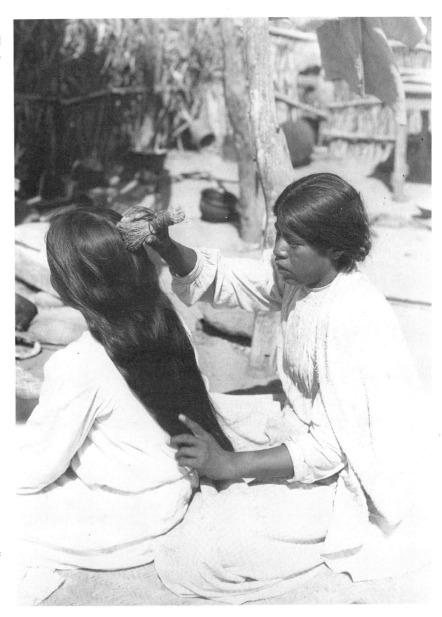

Right: A woman of the Pima tribe brushing a girl's hair.

Once a week, Pima Indians plastered their hair with mud and gum and left it on overnight. This killed the lice and made their hair shine when they had washed it with amole suds.

A "roach" is a crest of turkey beard or dyed deer hair which some Indian men wore tied in their hair.

tribes, it was customary for a man to comb and dress his wife's hair each morning.

Headgear

Feathers or fur were placed in the hair or on the head to tell people what deeds an Indian brave had performed. The familiar warbonnet headdress with rows of feathers originated among the tribes of the eastern woodlands and spread west across the plains. The Sioux had particularly splendid creations.

The foundation of a feather headdress was a skullcap made of deer or buffalo hide. Black-tipped tail feathers of two-year-old golden eagles were attached to it by loops at the base. A thong halfway up kept them properly aligned. A brow-band decorated with quills, talons, or beads ran from ear to ear. Ribbons or strips of ermine hung down from the ends. The whole thing was fastened securely by a

When a Hidatsa brave needed to capture some eagle feathers for his war-bonnet, he hid in a shallow pit. It was covered over with brushwood and a piece of meat was placed on it as bait. When the bird landed to take the meat, the man would try to pull out its tail feathers.

The Sioux were
famous for their
warbonnets made
of eagle feathers.
The Haida wove
hats from split
spruce roots.

45

thin strap under the chin.

For ordinary, everyday wear and for protection from the sun, wind, and rain, many tribes made hats of straw, bark, or animal skins. The women of some northwest coastal tribes wove ceremonial hats from split spruce roots and painted designs on them.

Jewelry

Both men and women wore jewelry, according to the customs of their tribes. Some pierced their ears and wore earrings made from shells or beads. Others wore rings or pins through a hole in their nostrils. These pins could be up to eight inches long. Labrets,

Phoebe Maddux of the Karok tribe was photographed in 1928 wearing a woven basketry cap, necklaces of dentalium shells and an apron of clam shells decorated with abalone pendants.

The Ojibwa and the Chippewa are the same tribe; there are two ways of spelling their name. The Ottawas were a sub-division of the Ojibwa, who gave their name to the city of Ottawa. Ottawa used to be called Ottaway which means "traders." In the early seventeenth century, there were probably 35,000 members of the Ojibwa tribe. An approximately similar number were living on U.S. reservations in 1985, with another 44,000 in Canada.

Necklace decorated with claws, beads and embroidery.

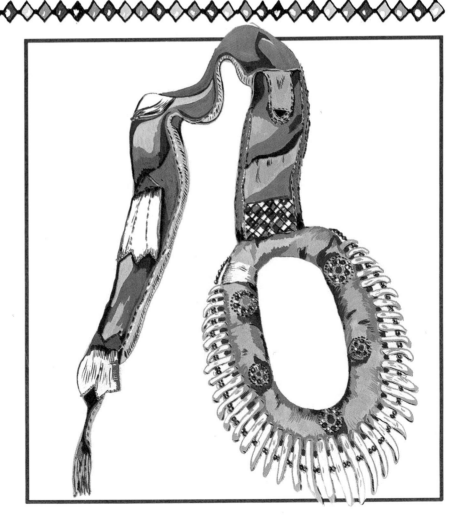

which stretched out the lower lip, were worn among the women of British Columbia. A hole was bored in the lip and plugged with an oval piece of wood. The plug could be as much as two inches long and an inch wide. Bracelets, anklets, rings, and necklaces were made of silver, copper, seeds, beads, shells, claws, teeth, and bones, depending on what was available locally or what could be traded.

Blankets

Linen and cotton were generally unknown to the Indians, and most tribes had little wool. Some tribes in northern Canada spun the wool of wild mountain goats and wove it into blankets. Because this wool was difficult to get, they twisted yarn for the background with strands of cedar bark or narrow strips of sea otter skin.

To make one blanket, a weaver needed the wool

Pueblo women carding, spinning and weaving blankets.

48

Stones keep the warp threads taut as a woman weaves a blanket in the typical Chilkat style.

from three goats. The wool was carefully sorted, so that the finest and softest was used. It was twisted into yarn and wound into balls ready for weaving. The blankets had complicated designs which were usually meant to represent animals. The weavers

used three main colors: black, yellow, and turquoise. The men designed the patterns and drew them on boards made of cedar. The women wove them on a simple frame loom. The warp threads were hung from a cross beam strengthened with two vertical

The weavers of the Chilkat tribe used stylized designs representing animals. This cloak is typical.

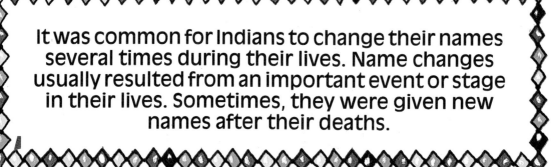

It was common for Indians to change their names several times during their lives. Name changes usually resulted from an important event or stage in their lives. Sometimes, they were given new names after their deaths.

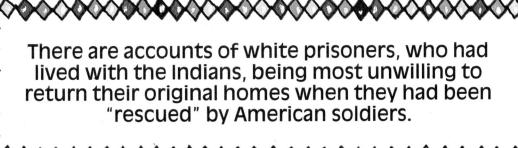
There are accounts of white prisoners, who had lived with the Indians, being most unwilling to return their original homes when they had been "rescued" by American soldiers.

poles. Because the blankets took many hours to make, they were highly valued and were used only on special occasions by important people.

The Coast Salish tribes raised a special breed of small white dogs especially for their wool, which was made into blankets. These dogs are now extinct.

Women from other tribes along the coast of British Columbia wove twisted strips of shredded cedar bark to make aprons, cloaks, and dresses which were soft and warm.

The women of the eastern woodlands used a very simple form of weaving. They cut rabbit skins round and round in a spiral with the fur still on them, so that they formed long strips about half an inch wide. These strips were joined together, twisted, and rolled into a large ball. This ball could then be woven in and out of the warp set up on a square frame to make a soft, warm, lightweight sheet which could be used as a sleeping robe or made into clothing.

Among the Pueblo Indians, the men traditionally did the weaving and embroidery. Their wool blankets, which are still made today, are usually striped. The Pueblo tribes have also woven cotton since prehistoric times.

Some of the most famous Indian blankets are those made by the women of the Navajo tribe. The wool is sheared, carded, washed in yucca suds, and spun on a traditional wooden spindle. The yarn may

need to be spun several times before it is fine and strong enough.

A vertical loom is set up outdoors on a pole frame. The weaver kneels down in front of it and works up from the bottom of the frame. She passes the weft threads through the warp with her fingers, helped by a small rod, but no shuttle. Mineral and vegetable dyes give the blankets a rich variety of color, and the designs are generally geometric.

Leather and fur

Among most tribes, the majority of the clothing was made of leather or fur. In the colder areas, beautifully made garments were carefully sewn from the skins of many animals. Indian women, especially those of the Plains tribes, were also very skilled at tanning and curing. Tanning was very important, and a women was judged by her ability to get good results. A skilled tanner knew how to make soft leather for clothing from the skins of beaver, marmot, squirrel, rabbit, buffalo, elk, moose, deer, and antelope.

First, the hide was either staked out on the ground or tied to an upright frame. All the flesh, and usually the hair as well, was carefully scraped from the skin with a stone scraper. This was very hard and tiring work, which took a long time. Then, a tool made of horn with a flint blade was used to even out the hide to the same thickness all over.

Next, the skin was tanned by rubbing it with a

The Blackfeet may have gotten their tribal name because they wore black moccasins.

54

mixture of brains, sour milk, elm bark, and liver. When it was dry, the hide was soaked in water to clean it and then wrung dry and stretched over a frame to dry out completely. It then had to be scraped again on both sides and rubbed and pulled to make it soft. Tanning a skin took about a week.

It was then ready to be made into clothes. The women used a stone or copper knife to cut the shape of a garment, which they copied or remembered from watching their mothers when they were children. Then, they punched sewing holes with a bodkin and stitched the garments with a bone needle and with thread made from twisted animal sinew.

Garments

In most tribes, the men wore either long pants or breechcloths and leggings, and the women wore either a dress or a skirt. A breechcloth was a strip of soft, tanned leather. It was worn between the legs and draped over a belt at the front and back to hold it in place. Both sexes had robes or mantles which they wore for extra warmth and often slept in as well. The robe was worn sideways, with the tail to the right. It was tied over the left shoulder. Mittens were also worn when the weather was cold. Shirts for men were not usually everyday wear, but were kept for special ceremonial occasions.

When it was warm, children up to the age of seven or eight usually went naked. They did, however, wear moccasins where necessary to protect their feet from snakes and ants, and from sharp stones and thorns.

Most tribes loved to decorate their clothes. They painted and embroidered them by sewing on beads, shells, fringes, feathers, and porcupine quills. When the early white traders came, the Indians admired the bright colors of the soft fabrics which they brought with them. The traders, of course, valued the Indians' furs, particularly the sea otter cloaks of the Canadian Indians.

One item of Indian clothing which the white settlers adopted, and which many people still wear today, were moccasins, which were made in several different styles for varying uses.

By modern standards, an Indian home would probably be uncomfortable, crowded, and inconvenient to us. If we visited the house of an ordinary white family one hundred and fifty years ago, we would probably not like it much better. The Indian made good use of what was available at the time in his own locality. As opportunities for trade increased, a more modern and convenient way of life gradually developed. Nevertheless, some members of some tribes still maintain the style of their traditional homes today.

Mohave and Yuma boys were initiated into manhood at the age of ten. The nasal septum (the part of the nose which divides the nostrils) was pierced and a cord put in. For the next four days, the boy had to run ten to fifteen miles each day so that he covered north, south, east, and west. On the fourth day, the cord was removed, and a greasewood stick put in its place. Later, the stick was replaced by a string of beads.

Glossary

adobe   clay which can be shaped into bricks and dried by the sun

agriculturalist   a farmer

braided   plaited

cache   hiding place for food

caliche   dried stiff clay

cannibalism   humans eating other humans

ceremonial   used for special occasions, usually concerned with religion

climate   temperature, wind, and rainfall

diameter   the distance across a circle measured across the center

excavate   dig up

hogan   a house of the Navajo Indians

initiation   ceremonial test or trial by ordeal which allows a person to join a group or society

jerky   strips of dried meat

kiva   a building for religious ceremonies

mantle   a long sleeveless cloak

mortar and pestle   a bowl made from a hard substance, often marble, and a club-shaped tool which are used for grinding corn or ingredients for cooking

natural resource   something—animal, vegetable, or mineral—from the natural world which can be used

nomadic   wandering from place to place; having no settled dwelling

Glossary

nutritious food which is good for you

ocher a type of clay which contains iron and can be used to make a yellowish-brown paint

palisade a fence made of rails or posts

pemmican a food made from dried meat

pueblo Spanish word for "town;" a group of Indian buildings built from clay bricks

pump-drill a tool for lighting a fire

sinew the tough tissue of the body which joins the muscles to the bones

tipi or tepee tent made from buffalo hide; used by the Plains Indians

totem pole a carved and painted pole which showed a man's family history and importance

travois two tepee poles tied together in a V-shape which could be loaded with goods and pulled by a dog or a horse. "Travois" means "shaft" in French

utilized used

vermilion a bright red paint made from mercuric sulfide

warp the threads on a loom which are stretched lengthwise from top to bottom

weft the threads on a loom which are woven over and under the warp

wickiup a small house made from poles and dried grass which was not intended to last long

Table of Tribes

This list shows some of the most important Indian tribes of North America, the regions in which they lived and the languages spoken.

FAR NORTH

Algonquin; Macro-Algonkian
Beaver; Na-Dene
Beothuk; Language group unknown
Carrier; Na-Dene
Chilcotin; Na-Dene
Chipewyan; Na-Dene
Cree; Macro-Algonkian
Dogrib; Na-Dene
Hare; Na-Dene
Kaska; Na-Dene
Koyukon; Na-Dene
Kutchin; Na-Dene
Micmac; Macro-Algonkian
Montagnais; Macro-Algonkian
Naskapi; Macro-Algonkian
Ottawa; Macro-Algonkian
Sarsi; Na-Dene
Slave; Na-Dene
Tanaina; Na-Dene
Tutchone; Na-Dene
Yellowknife; Na-Dene

NORTHWEST COAST

Bella Coola; Language group unknown
Chilkat; Na-Dene
Chinook; Penutian
Coast Salish; Language group unknown
Haida; Na-Dene
Klikitat; Penutian
Kwakiutl; Language group unknown
Nootka; Language group unknown
Quileute; Language group unknown
Quinault; Language group unknown
Tlingit; Na-Dene
Tsimshian; Penutian

CALIFORNIA-INTERMOUNTAIN

Bannock; Aztec-Tanoan
Cayuse; Penutian
Chumash; Hokan
Diegueño; Hokan
Flathead; Language group unknown
Gabrielino; Aztec-Tanoan
Gosiute; Aztec-Tanoan
Hupa; Na-Dene
Interior Salish; Language group unknown

Karok; Hokan
Klamath; Penutian
Kutenai; Language group unknown
Maidu; Penutian
Modoc; Penutian
Mohave; Hokan
Nez Percé; Penutian
Paiute; Aztec-Tanoan
Pomo; Hokan
Shoshoni; Aztec-Tanoan
Ute; Aztec-Tanoan
Wintun; Penutian

SOUTHWEST

Apache; Na-Dene
Cochimi; Hokan
Havasupai; Hokan
Maricopa; Hokan
Navajo; Na-Dene
Papago; Aztec-Tanoan
Pima; Aztec-Tanoan
Pueblo:
   Acoma; Language group unknown
   Hopi; Aztec-Tanoan
   Laguna; Language group unknown
   San Ildefonso; Aztec-Tanoan
   Taos; Aztec-Tanoan
   Zia; Language group unknown
Zuñi; Language group unknown
Waiguri; Hokan
Yaqui; Aztec-Tanoan
Yuma; Hokan

PLAINS

Arapaho; Macro-Algonkian
Arikara; Macro-Siouan
Assiniboin; Macro-Siouan
Atakapa; Macro-Algonkian
Blackfeet:
   Blood; Macro-Algonkian
   Piegan; Macro-Algonkian
Caddo; Macro-Siouan
Cheyenne; Macro-Algonkian
Comanche; Aztec-Tanoan
Crow; Macro-Siouan
Gros Ventre; Macro-Algonkian
Hidatsa; Macro-Siouan

Iowa; Macro-Siouan
Kansa; Macro-Siouan
Karankawa; Language group
  unknown
Kiowa; Aztec-Tanoan
Mandan; Macro-Siouan
Missouri; Macro-Siouan
Omaha; Macro-Siouan
Osage; Macro-Siouan
Pawnee; Macro-Siouan
Ponca; Macro-Siouan
Quapaw; Macro-Siouan
Sioux; (Dakotah):
  Oglala; Macro-Siouan
  Santee; Macro-Siouan
  Sisseton; Macro-Siouan
  Teton; Macro-Siouan
  Yankton; Macro-Siouan
Wichita; Macro-Siouan

EASTERN WOODLANDS
Abnaki; Northeast; Macro-Algonkian
Calusa; Southeast; Macro-Siouan
Cherokee; Southeast; Macro-Siouan
Chickasaw; Southeast; Macro-Algonkian
Chippewa; Northeast & Far North;
  Macro-Algonkian
Chitimacha; Southeast; Macro-Algonkian

Choctaw; Southeast; Macro-Algonkian
Conestoga; Northeast; Macro-Siouan
Creek; Southeast; Macro-Algonkian
Delaware (Lenape); Northeast;
  Macro-Algonkian
Huron; Northeast; Macro-Siouan
Illinois; Northeast; Macro-Algonkian
Iroquois; Northeast; Macro-Siouan
Kickapoo; Northeast; Macro-Algonkian
Malecite; Northeast; Macro-Algonkian
Massachusetts; Northeast;
  Macro-Algonkian
Menominee; Northeast; Macro-Algonkian
Miami; Northeast; Macro-Algonkian
Missisauga; Northeast; Macro-Algonkian
Mohican; Northeast; Macro-Algonkian
Natchez; Southeast; Macro-Algonkian
Potawatomi; Northeast; Macro Algonkian
Powhatan; Southeast; Macro-Algonkian
Sauk; Northeast; Macro-Algonkian
Seminole;Southeast; Macro-Algonkian
Shawnee; Southeast; Macro-Algonkian
Timucua; Southeast; Language group
  unknown
Tuscarora; Southeast; Macro-Siouan
Wampanoag; Northeast; Macro-Algonkian
Winnebago; Northeast; Macro-Siouan

Tribal Areas

THE FAR NORTH AREA

Algonquin	Dogrib	Naskapi
Beaver	Hare	Ottawa
Beothuk	Kaska	Sarsi
Carrier	Koyukon	Slave
Chilcotin	Kutchin	Tanaina
Chipewyan	Micmac	Tutchone
Cree	Montagnais	Yellowknife

THE NORTHWEST COAST AREA

Chinook
Haida
Klikitat
Kwakiutl
Nootka
Quileute
Quinault
Tlingit
Tsimshian

CALIFORNIA-INTERMOUNTAIN

Bannock	Karok	Mohave
Cayuse	Klamath	Nez Percé
Chumash	Kutenai	Paiute
Flathead	Luiseno	Pomo
Gosiute	Maidu	Shoshoni
Hupa	Modoc	Ute
		Wintun

THE SOUTHWEST AREA

Apache	Laguna
Cochimi	San Ildefonso
Navajo	Taos
Papago	Zia
Pima	Zuñi
Pueblo:	Waiguri
Acoma	Yaqui
Hopi	Yuma

THE PLAINS AREA

Arapaho	Crow	Pawnee
Arikara	Gros Ventre	Ponca
Assiniboin	Hidatsa	Quapaw
Atakapa	Iowa	Sioux:
Blackfeet:	Kansa	Oglala
Blood	Karankawa	Santee
Plegan	Kiowa	Sisseton
Caddo	Mandan	Teton
Cheyenne	Omaha	Yankton
Comanche	Osaga	Wichita

THE EASTERN WOODLANDS AREA

NORTHEAST

Abnaki		
Chippewa	Massachusetts	
Delaware	Menominee	
Erie	Miami	
Fox	Mohegan	
Huron	Narraganset	Chitimacha
Illinois	Potawatomi	Choctaw
Iroquois:	Sauk	Creek
Cayuga	Susquehanna	Natchez
Mohawk	Wampanoag	Powhatan
Onondaga	Winnebago	Seminole
Oneida		Shawnee
Seneca	SOUTHEAST	Timucua
Kickapoo	Calusa	Tuscarora
Mahican	Cherokee	Yamasee
Malecite	Chickasaw	Yuchi

The major linguistic areas

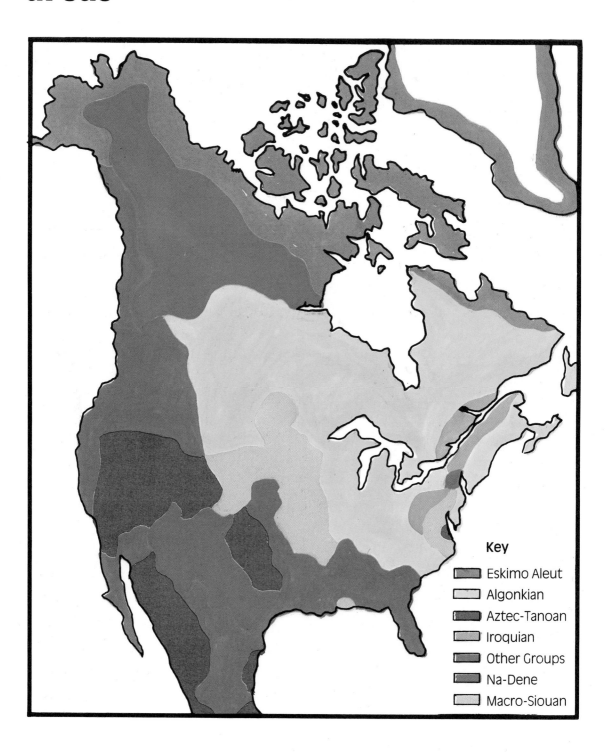

Key

Eskimo Aleut
Algonkian
Aztec-Tanoan
Iroquian
Other Groups
Na-Dene
Macro-Siouan

Index

Index of tribes